SPORTS SUPERSTARS

DIANA TAURASI

BY REBECCA SABELKO

TORQUE

BELLWETHER MEDIA · MINNEAPOLIS, MN

Torque brims with excitement perfect for thrill-seekers of all kinds. Discover daring survival skills, explore uncharted worlds, and marvel at mighty engines and extreme sports. In *Torque* books, anything can happen. Are you ready?

This edition first published in 2023 by Bellwether Media, Inc.

No part of this publication may be reproduced in whole or in part without written permission of the publisher. For information regarding permission, write to Bellwether Media, Inc., Attention: Permissions Department, 6012 Blue Circle Drive, Minnetonka, MN 55343.

Library of Congress Cataloging-in-Publication Data

LC record for Diana Taurasi available at: https://lccn.loc.gov/2022050059

Text copyright © 2023 by Bellwether Media, Inc. TORQUE and associated logos are trademarks and/or registered trademarks of Bellwether Media, Inc.

Editor: Kieran Downs   Designer: Josh Brink

Printed in the United States of America, North Mankato, MN.

TABLE OF CONTENTS

TAURASI'S GOT 30!	4
WHO IS DIANA TAURASI?	6
GETTING INTO THE GAME	8
A SUPERSTAR!	12
TAURASI'S FUTURE	20
GLOSSARY	22
TO LEARN MORE	23
INDEX	24

TAURASI'S GOT 30!

The Phoenix Mercury are taking on the Los Angeles Sparks. Early on, Diana Taurasi hits an easy **3-pointer**. At halftime, the Mercury are up by 22 points.

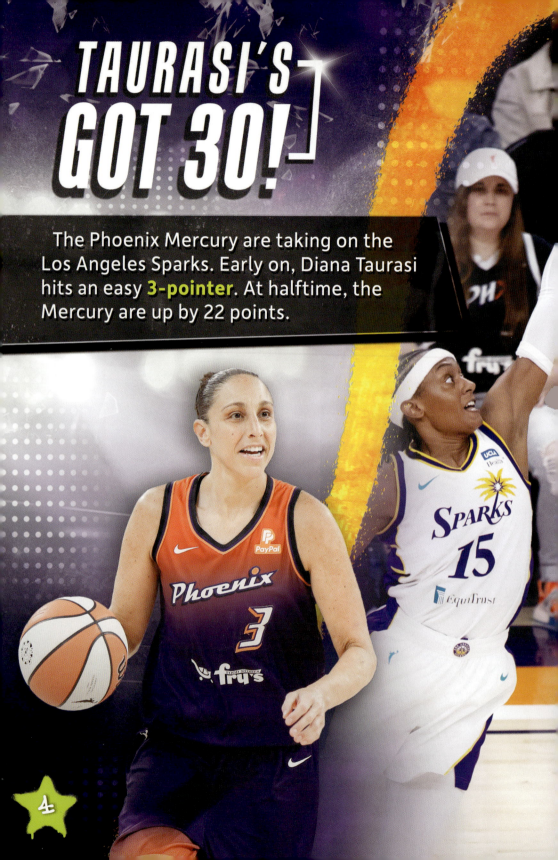

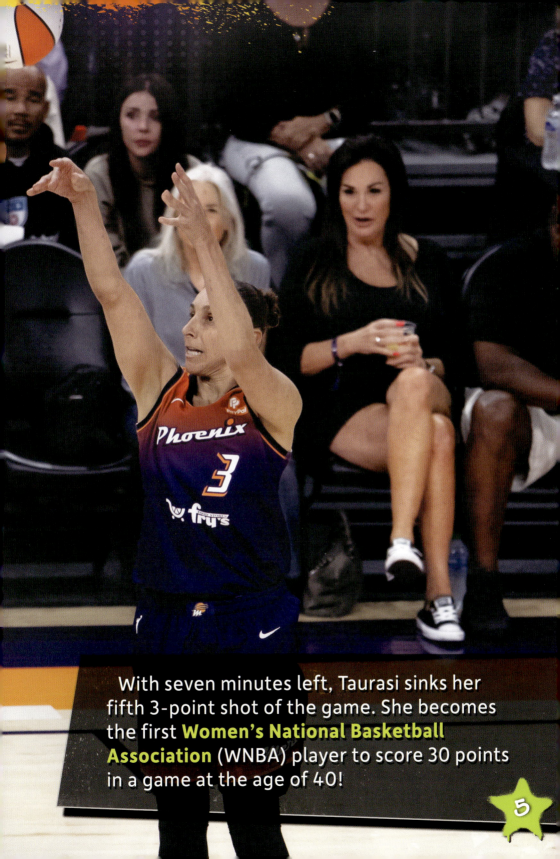

With seven minutes left, Taurasi sinks her fifth 3-point shot of the game. She becomes the first **Women's National Basketball Association** (WNBA) player to score 30 points in a game at the age of 40!

WHO IS DIANA TAURASI?

Diana Taurasi is a **guard** for the WNBA's Phoenix Mercury. Taurasi has also played for Team USA in five **Olympic Games**. She has been on many European teams, too.

DIANA TAURASI

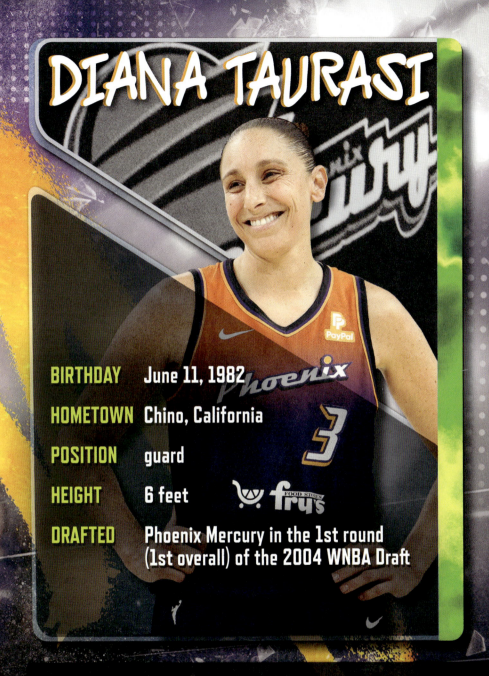

BIRTHDAY June 11, 1982

HOMETOWN Chino, California

POSITION guard

HEIGHT 6 feet

DRAFTED Phoenix Mercury in the 1st round (1st overall) of the 2004 WNBA Draft

Taurasi is often called one of the best basketball players of all time. She has helped the Mercury win three WNBA **championships**. She has also been named the WNBA's **Most Valuable Player** (MVP).

7

GETTING INTO THE GAME

Taurasi grew up in Chino, California. She loved to play soccer and basketball. But she knew she had more of a future in basketball.

TAURASI IN HIGH SCHOOL

A Special Visit

When Diana was in high school, UCONN's coach visited Diana and her family. He did this to show how much he wanted her to play for the Huskies.

Taurasi was a standout player at an early age. Beginning in middle school, she won awards for her talent. She broke records in high school. She became one of the top players in the country.

Taurasi started playing for the University of Connecticut Huskies in 2000. In her second year, she led the team to a perfect 39–0 season. The team won the national championship!

Taurasi continued to work hard and improve. She led the Huskies to two more championships. She also earned two National Player of the Year awards. Taurasi was ready for the WNBA!

2004 WOMEN'S NATIONAL CHAMPION

FAVORITES

OTHER SPORT

soccer

BASKETBALL PLAYER

Magic Johnson

HOBBY

ironing

CARTOON

Duck Tales

A Winning Team
The Huskies won 139 regular season games in the 4 years Taurasi was on the team. They only had 8 losses.

A SUPERSTAR!

The Phoenix Mercury needed a leader after a terrible 2003 season. They **drafted** Taurasi as the number one pick in 2004. She won the **Rookie** of the Year award that season.

2004 WNBA DRAFT

DIANA TAURASI MAP

- Phoenix Mercury, Phoenix, Arizona — 2004 to present
- Team USA, Colorado Springs, Colorado — 2004 to 2021

2020 TOKYO OLYMPICS

Taurasi also played in the 2004 Olympics. She helped Team USA win a gold medal. She has won four more golds since her first Olympic Games!

Taurasi quickly proved she was a basketball superstar. She led the WNBA in scoring in 2006. She set a WNBA record after scoring 47 points in one game.

The Mercury were set for a winning 2007 season with Taurasi as their leader. She drove the team through the **Finals** to their first championship win!

2007 WNBA CHAMPION

Taurasi showed her strong play in 2009. She led the WNBA in points per game and 3-pointers. She earned the WNBA MVP award. After another championship win, she was also crowned the Finals MVP.

Season after season, Taurasi put out big numbers and rarely missed games. But a hip injury in 2012 cost her the season.

2009 WNBA CHAMPION

2014 WNBA CHAMPION AND FINALS MVP

TIMELINE

Phoenix
— 2004 —
Taurasi is drafted by the Mercury

— 2007 —
Taurasi wins her first WNBA Championship

Taurasi returned strong and ready to play in the 2013 season. She led the team to the Finals. Then in 2014, the Mercury won their third championship title. Taurasi was awarded the Finals MVP once again.

Since then, Taurasi continues to be a top player. She became the WNBA's leader in **career** points in 2017!

So Many Points!
Taurasi finished the 2022 season with 9,693 career regular season points!

— 2014 —
Taurasi wins her third WNBA Championship

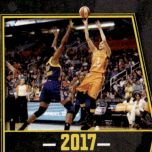

— 2017 —
Taurasi becomes the WNBA record holder in career points

— 2021 —
Taurasi is voted as the WNBA's greatest player of all time

TAURASI'S FUTURE

Taurasi has had a long, amazing WNBA career. In 2021, fans voted her as the WNBA's best player of all time!

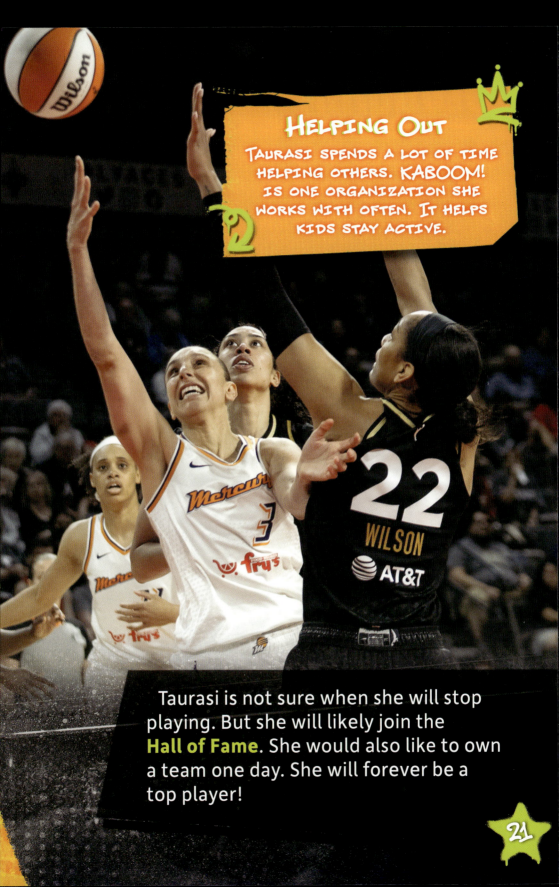

Helping Out

Taurasi spends a lot of time helping others. KABOOM! is one organization she works with often. It helps kids stay active.

Taurasi is not sure when she will stop playing. But she will likely join the **Hall of Fame**. She would also like to own a team one day. She will forever be a top player!

GLOSSARY

3-pointer—a shot taken from behind a line that counts for three points instead of two

career—related to the job that a person has for most of their professional life

championships—contests to decide the best team or person

drafted—chose by a process during which professional teams choose high school and college players to play for them

Finals—the championship series of the Women's National Basketball Association

guard—a player who is often smaller than other players on the team and good at ball handling and shooting

Hall of Fame—a place honoring the records of top people in a sport

most valuable player—the best player in a year, game, or series; the most valuable player is often called the MVP.

Olympic Games—worldwide summer or winter sports contests held in a different country every four years

rookie—a first-year player in a sports league

Women's National Basketball Association—a league for professional basketball in the United States; the Women's National Basketball Association is often called the WNBA.

TO LEARN MORE

AT THE LIBRARY

Adamson, Thomas K. *Basketball Records*. Minneapolis, Minn.: Bellwether Media, 2018.

Downs, Kieran. *LeBron James*. Minneapolis, Minn.: Bellwether Media, 2023.

Kelley, K.C. *WNBA Superstars*. Mankato, Minn.: The Child's World, 2020.

ON THE WEB

FACTSURFER

Factsurfer.com gives you a safe, fun way to find more information.

1. Go to www.factsurfer.com

2. Enter "Diana Taurasi" into the search box and click 🔍.

3. Select your book cover to see a list of related content.

INDEX

awards, 7, 9, 10, 12, 13, 16, 17, 18, 19, 20
championships, 7, 10, 15, 16, 18, 19
childhood, 8, 9
Chino, California, 8
drafted, 12
favorites, 11
Finals, 15, 16, 18, 19
future, 8, 21
guard, 6
Hall of Fame, 21
injury, 16
KABOOM!, 21
map, 13
Most Valuable Player, 7, 16, 18, 19
Olympic Games, 6, 13
Phoenix Mercury, 4, 6, 7, 12, 15, 19
profile, 7
records, 9, 14, 19
Rookie of the Year, 12
scoring, 4, 5, 14, 16, 19
soccer, 8
Team USA, 6, 13
timeline, 18–19
trophy shelf, 17
University of Connecticut Huskies, 9, 10, 11
Women's National Basketball Association, 5, 6, 7, 10, 12, 14, 15, 16, 18, 19, 20

The images in this book are reproduced through the courtesy of: Rick Scuteri/ AP Newsroom, front cover (hero); Michele Morrone, p. 3; Icon Sportswire, pp. 4, 4-5; Christian Petersen/ Getty Images, pp. 6-7, 7, 16, 17, 19 (2017), 20; Danny Raustadt, p. 7 (Mercury logo); Al Schaben/ Getty Images, p. 8; Jeff Gross/ Getty Images, p. 9; Elsa/ Getty Images, pp. 10, 11; FocusStocker, p. 11 (other sport); Debby Wong, p. 11 (basketball player); Stanislav Khokholkov, p. 11 (hobby); Moviestore Collection Ltd/ Alamy, p. 11 (cartoon); BILL KOSTROUN/ AP Newsroom, pp. 12, 18 (2004); BCFC, p. 13 (Phoenix, Arizona); USA Basketball Youth Development Guidebook/ Wiki Commons, p. 13 (Colorado Springs, Colorado); Tim Clayton - Corbis/ Getty Images, p. 13; Francis Specker/ Alamy, p. 14; Jerry S. Mendoza/ AP Newsroom, p. 15; KAMIL KRZACZYNSKI/ AP Newsroom, pp. 18-19; WENN/ Alamy, p. 18 (2007); Ellen Schmidt/ AP Newsroom, p. 21; Keeton10, p. 23.